Conserving Resources

Orlando Austin New York San Diego Toronto London

Visit *The Learning Site!*
www.harcourtschool.com

Lesson 1

What Are Some Types of Resources?

VOCABULARY

resource
renewable resources
reusable resources
nonrenewable resources

A **resource** is something found in nature that is used by living things. Trees are a resource.

Renewable resources are resources that can be replaced during a person's lifetime. Animals are renewable resources.

Reusable resources are resources that can be used again and again. Water is a reusable resource.

Nonrenewable resources are resources that cannot be replaced. When they are used up, there will be no more. Oil is a nonrenewable resource.

READING FOCUS SKILL

MAIN IDEA AND DETAILS

The **main idea** is what the text is mostly about. **Details** tell more about the **main idea**. Look for **details** about resources.

Resources

A **resource** is something found in nature that is used by living things. Animals are resources. People use them for food and clothing. Plants are also resources. They are used for food and to make things, such as paper and clothes.

Grass is a resource for cows. Cows are a resource for people. ▼

Water is an important resource. So are air, rocks, metals, oil, and salt.

Resources are found in many places. Some resources are above ground. Others are below ground.

Focus Skill **Tell why plants and animals are resources.**

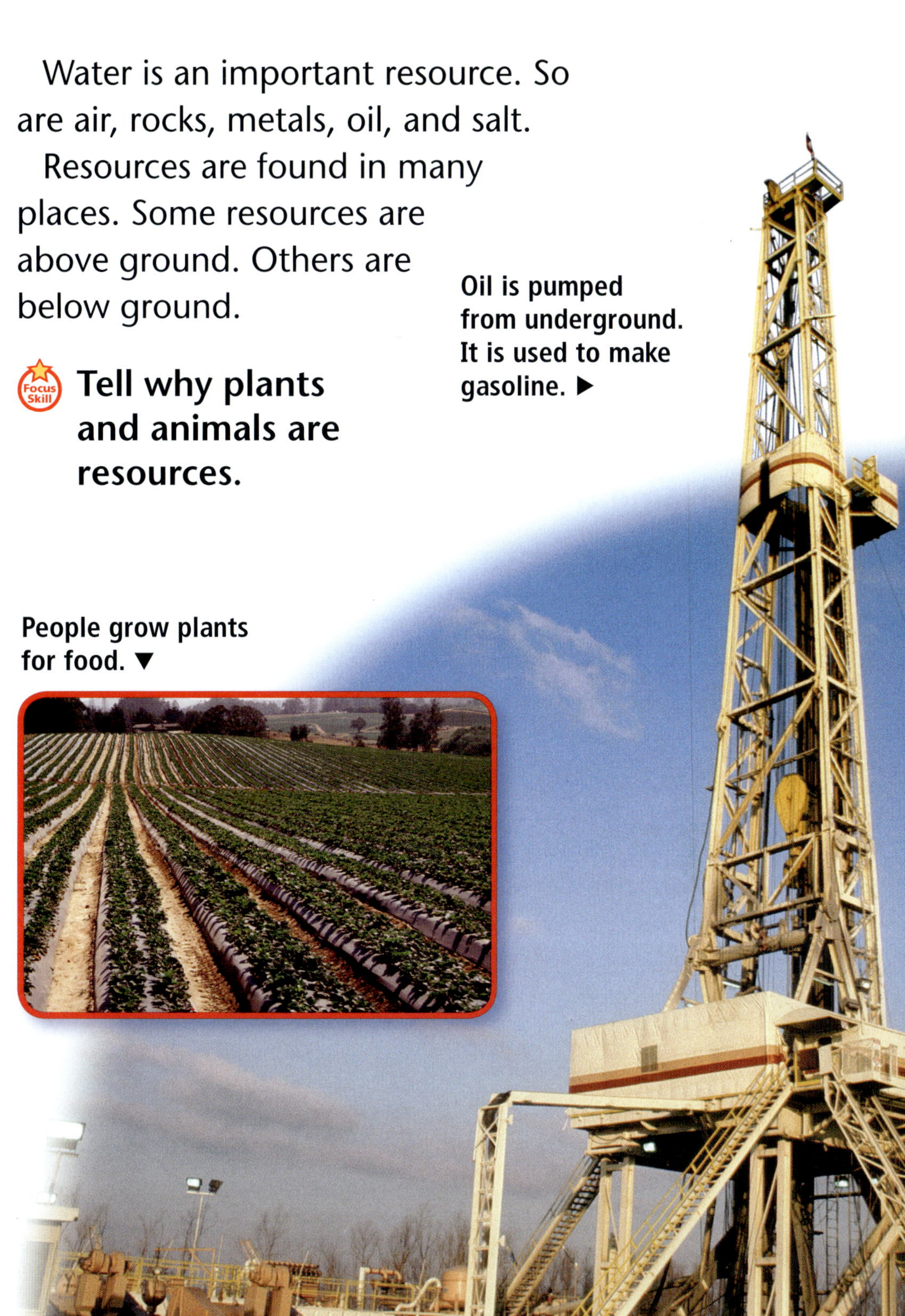

Oil is pumped from underground. It is used to make gasoline. ▶

People grow plants for food. ▼

Renewable Resources

Some resources can be replaced. Others cannot. **Renewable resources** can be replaced during a person's lifetime.

Plants and animals are renewable resources. Some kinds of energy are renewable resources, too. Energy from the sun is a renewable resource.

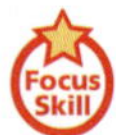

Focus Skill **Name three renewable resources.**

Trees are renewable resources.

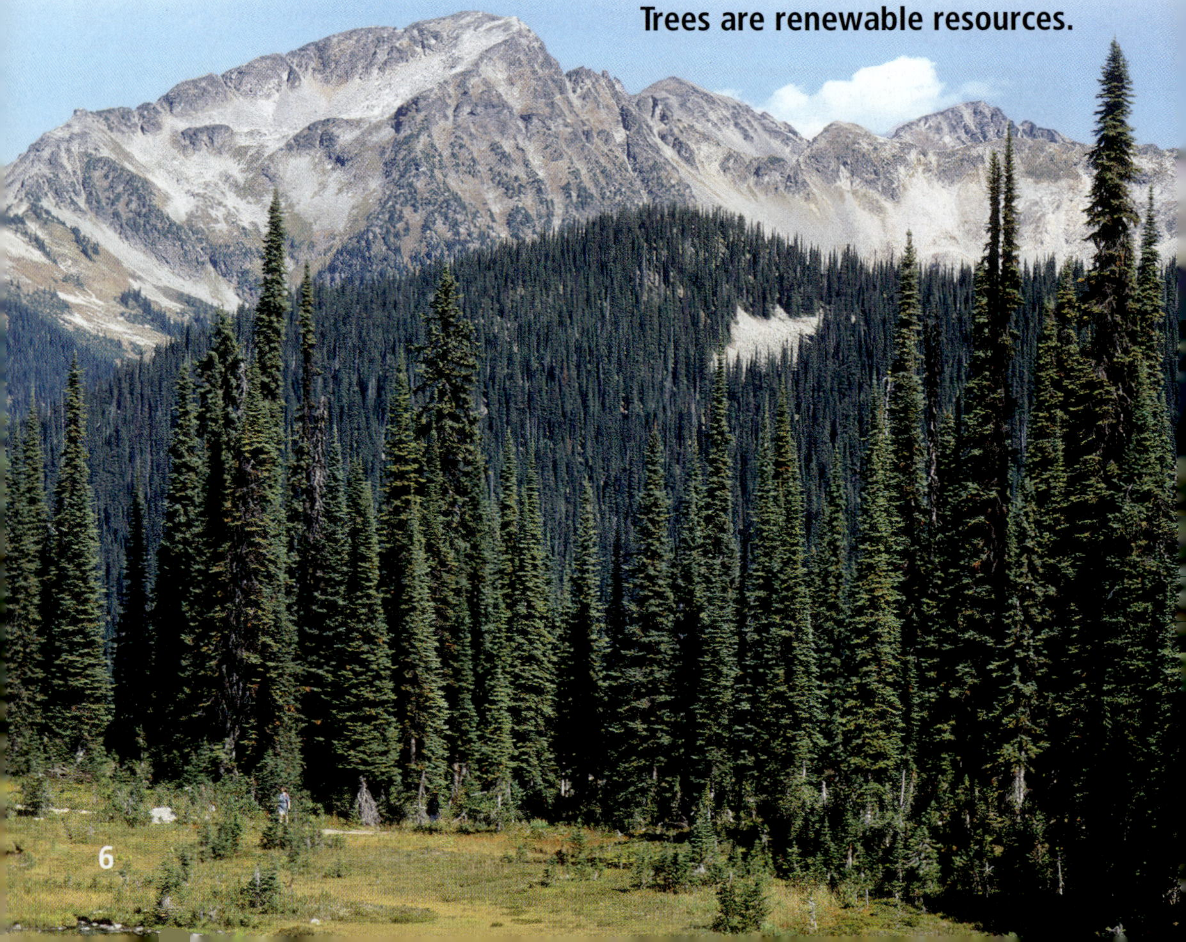

Reusable Resources

Reusable resources can be used again and again. Air and water are two reusable resources.

After water is used, it is polluted. A water treatment plant can clean water. Then it can be used again.

Cars and factories can pollute the air. Plants, wind, and rain help clean the air. Then it is safe to breathe again.

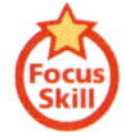

Focus Skill **What are some kinds of reusable resources?**

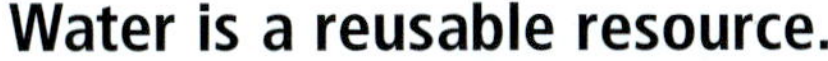

Water is a reusable resource.

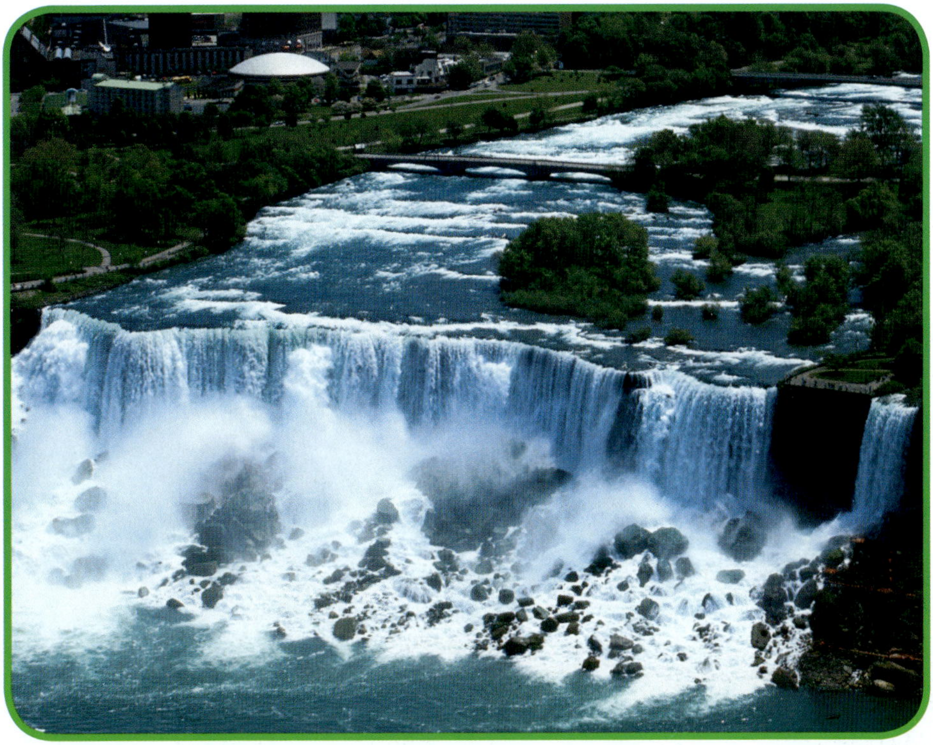

Nonrenewable Resources

Nonrenewable resources are resources that cannot be replaced. When they are used up, there will be no more.

Gasoline is a nonrenewable resource. One day the oil used to make gas will all be gone. Coal, soil, and metals are also nonrenewable resources.

What are some nonrenewable resources?

▼ **Metal is often dug out of the ground.**

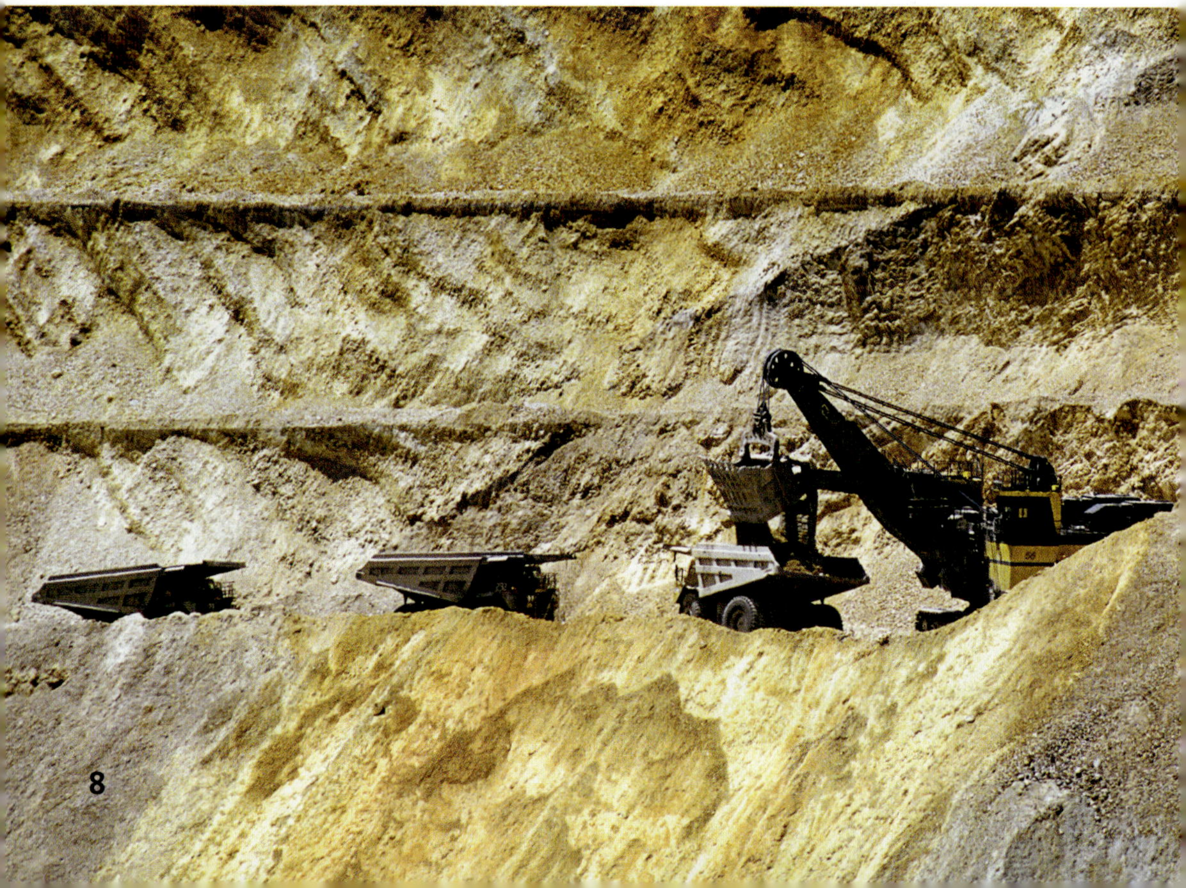

▲ Coal takes thousands of years to form. People dig it out of the ground.

Review

Complete this main idea statement.

1. Living things use many kinds of ______ in order to live.

Complete these detail sentences.

2. ______ resources can be replaced.
3. Water and air are ______ resources that can be used again and again.
4. A ______ resource, such as metal, cannot be replaced.

Lesson 2

What Are Some Types of Soil?

VOCABULARY

humus
sand
silt
clay
loam

Humus is the part of soil made up of bits of dead plants and animals.

Sand is soil with grains of rock that you can see with your eyes. Sand covers many beaches.

Silt is soil with grains of rock that are too small to see with your eyes.

Clay is soil with very, very tiny grains of rock.

Loam is soil that is a mixture of humus, sand, silt, and clay. Loam is used to grow fruits and vegetables.

READING FOCUS SKILL

COMPARE AND CONTRAST

When you **compare and contrast**, you tell how things are alike and different.

Look for ways to **compare and contrast** types of soil.

Layers of Soil

Soil is an important resource. Plants need soil to grow. Many animals live in soil.

Soil is a mixture. It is made up of water, air, tiny rocks, and humus. **Humus** is made up of bits of dead plants and animals.

Plants grow in soil. ▼

Soil forms in layers. Soil near the top has a lot of humus. Deeper down, soil has less humus and more rocks.

Focus Skill **Tell how soil near the surface is different from soil deeper down.**

Different Types of Soil

There are many kinds of soil. Soils have different colors. Some soils hold more water than others. Soils also have different sizes of rocks in them. The rock sizes make the soil feel different.

Sandy soil ▼

Clay soil has tiny grains of rock.

There are three main types of soil. The main difference among them is the size of rocks in them.

Sand is soil with grains of rock that you can see with your eyes. **Silt** is soil with grains of rock too small to see with your eyes. **Clay** is soil with very, very tiny grains of rock.

Focus Skill **Tell how sand, silt, and clay soils are alike and different.**

The Importance of Soil

Soil is important to many living things. Plants grow in soil. Many animals make their homes in soil.

Farmers use soil to grow crops. ▼

Soil is also important to people. We use soil to make bricks and pottery. We also use soil to grow many foods. **Loam** is the best soil to grow crops. Loam is a mixture of humus, clay, silt, and sand.

▲ **Most crops are grown in loam.**

Tell different ways people use soil.

Review

Complete these compare and contrast statements.

1. All kinds of soil are an important ______.
2. The top layer of soil usually has more ______ than the other layers.
3. The grains of rock in ______ are larger than those in silt.
4. ______ is soil that has the smallest grains of rock.

VOCABULARY

pollution

How Do People Use and Impact the Environment?

Pollution is any harmful material in the environment. Smoke can cause air pollution.

READING FOCUS SKILL

CAUSE AND EFFECT

A **cause** is what makes something happen. An **effect** is what happens.

Look for some **effects** of people on the environment.

Uses of the Land

People use land in different ways. People build on land. They use resources from land, such as wood, rock, and metal, to make buildings.

People also use land to grow plants. Plants are used for food and to make medicine and cloth.

Many people live and work on land. ▼

Trees help hold soil in place. ▶

When people use land, they change it. Sometimes they change it in good ways. For example, planting trees can help hold soil in place.

Other times, people change land in bad ways. Mining can destroy land. It can harm plants and animals that live there.

Tell how people cause changes to land.

Mining for metals can harm land. ▼

Land Pollution

People also change land in bad ways when they make pollution. **Pollution** is any harmful material in the environment.

▼ Land pollution

Many things can cause pollution. Solid wastes, gases, and noise can cause pollution.

One kind of pollution is land pollution. People throwing trash in the wrong places causes land pollution.

Land pollution can harm plants, animals, and people. It can also make water dirty.

Tell what causes land pollution.

Some trash takes years to break down.

Air Pollution

Pollution can also harm air. Smoke from cars and factories causes most air pollution.

Air pollution can make it hard for people to breathe. It can also change the weather. Smoke traps heat from sunlight. This makes Earth warmer.

What causes air pollution?

◀ Polluted air

Clean air ▶

Water Pollution

Pollution can harm water, too. Trash and oil dumped in water can cause water pollution.

Polluted water is not safe to drink. It can make animals sick. Some water pollution can be cleaned up. Water treatment plants can make polluted water clean again.

Tell what can happen when water is polluted.

Oil spills cause water pollution. ▶

Review

Focus Skill **Complete these cause and effect statements.**

1. When people use land, they ______ it in some way.
2. Throwing trash in the wrong place can cause ______ pollution.
3. Air pollution can make it hard for people to ______ .
4. When water is polluted, it is unsafe to ______.

How Can Resources Be Used Wisely?

VOCABULARY

conservation
reduce
reuse
recycle

Conservation is saving resources by using them wisely. Writing on both sides of paper saves trees.

Reduce means to use less of a resource. Turning off a light when you are not using it reduces the use of electiricity.

Reuse means to use a resource again and again. Bags can be reused in many ways.

Recycle means to make new things from old things. Plastic bottles and old tires can be recycled to make a playground.

READING FOCUS SKILL
MAIN IDEA AND DETAILS

A **main idea** is what the text is mostly about. **Details** tell more about the main idea.

Look for **details** about how to save resources.

Protecting Resources

People use many resources. Some resources cannot be replaced when they are used up. So it is important to protect them. Conservation is one way to do this. **Conservation** is saving resources by using them wisely.

Tell why it is important to protect resources.

Conservation protects resources, such as water and animals. ▼

◀ Turning off lights reduces the use of electricity.

Reduce

One way to save resources is to use less of them, or reduce how much you use. To **reduce** resources means to use less of things.

There are many ways to reduce. You can take a shower instead of a bath. This saves water. You can ride a bike instead of using a car. This saves gas. Reducing now means there will be more resources for the future.

Tell how to reduce the amount of resources used.

Riding bikes reduces the use of gasoline. ▶

Reuse

Another way to save resources is to reuse them. **Reuse** means to use a resource again and again. When you reuse things, you need fewer new things made from resources. Reusing saves money, too.

Tell why it is important to reuse resources.

▼ Reusing bags to make gift wrap saves trees.

Recycle

Recycling also saves resources. Recycle means to break something down and use it to make something new. You can recycle paper, glass, metal, and plastic. Paper is recycled to make cards, paper towels, and newspaper. Plastic can be recycled to make park benches.

▲ Recycling symbol

What materials can be recycled?

Review

Focus Skill

Complete this main idea statement.

1. ______ helps protect Earth's resources.

Complete these detail statements.

2. Riding bikes helps ______ the use of gasoline.
3. When you ______ a resource, you use it again and again.
4. You can make something new when you ______ paper, glass, or plastic.

GLOSSARY

clay (KLAY) soil with very, very tiny grains of rock

conservation (kahn•ser•VAY•shuhn) saving resources by using them wisely

humus (HYOO•muhs) the part of soil made up of broken-down parts of dead plants and animals

loam (LOHM) soil that is a mixture of humus, sand, silt, and clay

nonrenewable resource (nahn•rih•NOO•uh•buhl REE•sawrs) a resource that cannot be replaced before more can be made

pollution (puh•LOO•shuhn) any harmful material in the environment

recycle (ree•SY•kuhl) to reuse a resource by breaking it down and making a new product

reduce (ree•DOOS) to use less of a resource

renewable resource (rih•NOO•uh•buhl REE•sawrs) a resource that can be replaced quickly

resource (REE•sawrs) a material that is found in nature and that is used by living things

reusable resource (ree•YOOZ•uh•buhl REE•sawrs) a resource that can be used again and again

reuse (ree•YOOZ) to use a resource again and again

sand (SAND) soil with grains of rock that you can see with your eyes

silt (SILT) soil with grains of rock that are too small to see with your eyes